3 - 1988

To Danie ♡ P9-BJO-172
from Grandmom L.
with Lots of Love!
♡ ♡

The Original
TOOTH FAIRY STORY

by Carl E. Miner

Illustrations by Melva Teeter

THE ORIGINAL TOOTH FAIRY STORY
Carl E. Miner - Author

Published by Children's Ventures, Inc.
P.O. Box 3000
Grants Pass, Oregon
March, 1986

Library of Congress Catalog Card Number 85-73462

ISBN 0-9615985-0-6

Printed in the United States of America

This book is dedicated to My Children:

Robin
Biff
Rusty
Carl

and to all of the children who have given their youth to build love between themselves and their Moms and Dads.

Carl E. Miner

r. Russell sat in his rocking chair, enjoying the early evening sun. There were still several hours of daylight left. This was the time of day when the bright light of the sun started turning to the glow of yellow, the time of day which signaled the end of the hustle and bustle, leaving time to relax, think and enjoy the hours before dark with favored memories.

Mr. Russell had finished his supper. Familiar sounds of dishes clattering came from the kitchen where Mrs. Russell was busily preparing the house for the end of another day. She hummed ever so softly as she went about her chores. Mr. Russell looked down at Winnie, sitting there with her tail wagging, and he knew that she was ready for their evening walk.

" "**M**rs. Russell," said Mr. Russell, in the tone that always made Winnie jump up and start her "I'm-ready-to-go" prance. "We're going for our walk now." Off they started, up the soft, rolling hills, through the wooded area, and out among the butter-flies, birds, and the soft scent of wildflowers.

Mr. Russell made a point never to go the same way twice. He often laughed when he returned home, telling Mrs. Russell that he always went a different way every evening so that he wouldn't leave an ugly, brown path to spoil Mother Nature's beautiful green carpet.

Mr. Russell and Winnie went ever so softly and ever so quietly. Their presence never disturbed the birds, squirrels, or other wildlife, that seemed to sense there was no danger as they passed among them.

Then the strangest thing happened. As they walked up one of the hills, sounds that Mr. Russell had never heard before were coming from the other side. Slowly they walked to the top, and then stopped suddenly. Mr. Russell couldn't believe his eyes. In fact, he rubbed his eyes just to be sure he was actually seeing what he saw.

There it was — an endless castle, built in the most peaceful valley he had ever seen. Mr. Russell had seen pictures of castles before, but never one like this. The color was white — white like snow . . . no! White like a child's tooth! Sure enough, all those thousands of blocks used to build the castle were shaped like children's teeth, and the cement holding them in place was the color of the blue in the sky. As the sun hit upon the castle, there was just a faint, golden sparkle coming from the sky-blue cement; and there around the castle were little elves working busily.

Mr. Russell dropped down on a large rock, and Winnie sat down in front of him. They just sat there and looked. All of a sudden Mr. Russell looked around and standing there was . . . Mr. Russell wasn't sure. It was bigger than the elves working down at the castle, but it was small. Mr. Russell thought, "Who could this be?" Before Mr. Russell could give much more thought to what was standing there, it spoke. Mr. Russell had never heard a voice so clear. It was not loud, not soft, not high, and not low. Every word rang like the clear, crisp chime of a bell but came to his ears like a soft, summer breeze. Mr. Russell just sat there and listened to every word.

" "I'm glad you came; I'm the Tooth Fairy. I'm sure you're wondering about me, my friends and our castle. If you would like, I will tell you about us."

Mr. Russell just nodded yes.

The Tooth Fairy continued. "Many years ago, we found this valley. It was quiet and peaceful, and we were alone at last. We decided this would be our home forever."

Mr. Russell followed every word the Tooth Fairy said.

"**Y**ou see," said the Tooth Fairy, "many years ago, as a child, I had a dream that I would find a valley of peace, and hidden in the valley of peace would be a cave, and in the cave would be coins, and the coins should be given to all the good little girls and boys all over the world. It was very difficult to determine if each little girl and boy was good, and I puzzled over the problem for a long time. Then I decided that the good children are supposed to brush their teeth at least twice a day. As children lose some teeth, and they put them under their pillows, I would silently slip in at night while they slept and look at their teeth. If they were good children and brushed their teeth regularly, they would be rewarded by the Tooth Fairy. That worked fine."

"One problem! Every morning when I returned home, I would have hundreds of sparkling white teeth. What was I to do with them? Finally, my wonderful little friends and I decided to build our castle just to honor all the good little girls and boys. As you can see, Mr. Russell, this is our castle to the children. Oh, yes, we take the teeth from all the girls and boys, sort them, and the bright, sparkling teeth become little bricks. The dull ones we grind up and add a dash of blue and a pinch of gold and use them to cement the other teeth together."

Mr. Russell sat spellbound in the warmth of his new friendship. He listened as the Tooth Fairy told him at one time, before they were forced to leave because of the cold winters, thousands of birds with feathers of crimson red had decorated the castle roof. As the red feathers dropped out, they were gathered by the elves and brought into the castle. Whenever the whitest of teeth were found under the little girl's or boy's pillow, the Tooth Fairy would not only leave some change, but a special reward — a crimson red feather.

Suddenly, Mr. Russell realized that the golden sunlight was fading into the dark blue of night and that Mrs. Russell would be worried if he didn't return soon. He said his farewells to the Tooth Fairy and started home.

That evening, lying all warm in their bed, with the tingle of sleep dancing around their room, Mr. Russell told Mrs. Russell all about Winnie and his evening walk. Mrs. Russell had heard many stories about their walks over the years. In fact, these lovely stories Mr. Russell told were often lost in the distance as sleep would overtake the words. But tonight, Mrs. Russell listened with a warm excitement as Mr. Russell finished his story; and sleep took over.

Then, ever so gently, Mrs. Russell touched Mr. Russell's hand, and the unspoken words of love were there.

Through the heart of a child passes the problems of the world. Only the texture of the heart can determine the speed.

Carl E. Miner